KING OF THE LIONS
and other animal stories
By Chairman Steve

KING OF THE LIONS
and other animal stories

Human though is manifested by animals, causing them to imitate humans in embarrassing and comical ways; therefore, we are the animals who should learn from the experiences of the animals in this book.

Chairman Steve is proud to admit he is Jewish. Like the lion, he cannot change from one species to another. Steve loves the Jewish people and hopes that they and all other people learn from any implications about the Jewish, as well as Catholic and Protestant religions.

No implication is intended against any religion that calls itself "science". Following Leo cannot be made a science if the moon is worshiped as a god. That is clearly lunacy.

There are other animal stories after the appendix following King of the Lions. The characters have no similar representation to those in the main story.

CONTENTS

I

1 Many years ago, the lion was held in great respect and awe;
He was a model of virtue and strength to all the others;
Most others stepped aside who saw them roam.

2 Other animals had a different mate every season;
Some even had many different mates every season;
Not so the lion. He stayed faithful to the same mate throughout all
his seasons.

3 The lion stayed chaste because of his great respect for the
moon.
The lion loved the moon.
He praised the moon every day.

4 He gave the moon another name.
That name was Diana.

5 A lion named Irving was considered a tzaddik or very righteous
and holy one,
And so greatly the moon he feared,
He roared his praise whenever it appeared.
He predicted the future by looking in her face
And was so overwhelmed by her charming grace,
When other lions gathered, he roared to them;
Instead of Diana, He called her, Hashem.

6 "A lioness shall have a cub,
Not knowing any other lion.
The cub shall splash 'round in our tub
And rule us with a hand of iron.
He will preach unto them
Who love Hashem
With mighty power.
Meeyowrr!"

II

1 There was once upon a time, a lioness of very noble character.
Her name was Marlene.
She knew no mate, because she saved herself for Diana.

2 She did all her own hunting, killing only when necessary.
Diana was kind to her
And provided food whenever she wanted it.
She hardly had to run more than a few steps to catch a rabbit or zebra.

3 Every night, she sat by a high cliff
Where she was exposed to the moon's rays on the bare rocks.

4 Whenever the moon rose, she roared at it,
"Diana, Diana, hear a call;
I know how much you love me and so I expect a miracle!"

5 Marlene had a cub there without knowing any mate
She named the cub, Leo.

6 Three lions followed a shooting star
That landed near Marlene and her cub.

7 "Did you see this lioness before?", one growled.

8 "I saw her hunting by herself in the evening
And roaring to the moon at night.
I never saw her with any other lion!", roared another.

9 "This must be the whelp of Diana!" roared a third.

10 Lions came to see him and give him presents, including a bone rattle and mink diaper.

11 They all roared, "This is wonderful!
Leo will be our king!
Let's lift our voice to sing;
The skies sing too, so thunderful!"

12 The singing was so loud
That even wolves in the nearby woodlands could hear it.
A young lion could hear the wolves growling among themselves.
He ran panting to Marlene.
"Into the grassland, the wolves are slipping
All lion cubs to shreds they are ripping!"

13 Marlene took Leo with her to the highest cliffs.
Though many cubs were killed,
The wolves did not get Leo.

III

1 Leo grew up in great stature and wisdom.
His mane was shaped like the star of Davy,
A king of the ancient lion nation.
He had a cousin named John, a whelp of Marlene's cousin, Liz.

2 Like a voice roaring in the wilderness,
John paced around the grasslands roaring, "Leo is coming!
The King of the Lions is coming!"

3 The lions all revered John and came to him.
They were glad to hear that they would have a king of their own.
Leo was among them.

4 With a broad leaf, John poured water on Leo's head and roared:
"King of the Lions thou art;
Now on! we must not part!"

5 And all of a sudden, Diana's love
Descended on Leo the form of a dove.

6 Then Leo began to roar:
"Together, rah! Let's score!
The time is very soon;
Animals will love the moon!
Animals must love all other animals as the moon above
Every animal must love.
And we must do her will:
No animal any other animal may kill!
Eat an animal?
Don't be a cannibal!"

7 "Like the skunk, I raise a stink:
We have lots of milk to drink
And lots of eggs to eat,
But eggs you must not beat,
Except unfertilized eggs,"
Leo begs.
"This must be our goal:
Destroy no living soul!"

8   This upset the other lions.
They expected that their king would lead them into battle against the wolves.

9 They roared, "We want meat!
Meat to eat!
There might not be enough milk and eggs for all of us!"

10 Leo roared, "I have meat to eat that you know not of:
My meat is to do Diana's will,
And better still:
My meat is to reflect Diana's love."

11 Other lions started after Leo and John.
Leo ran faster and got away.
John lagged behind.
The others grabbed John and bit his head off.

IV

1 Leo saw two lions,
Simple Simon and his brother Andy groping for fish at a river.

2 Leo roared, "Come with me and I will make you fishers of cats!"

3 Simple Simon became Leo's most loyal follower.
Leo took good care of him.
He licked Simon's feet whenever they became soiled.

4 Simple Simon was slow to learn,
But Leo had great patience.

5 Leo asked, "What is our moon's name?"

6 "Uh...Duh...Leo.", Simon answered.

7 "No, Diana!", Leo corrected him.

8 One day, Leo asked Simon,
"Who would you say I, a son of a cat, am?"

9 Replied Simon, "Uh...Duh...yyyou are the King of the Lions!"

10 Leo was very pleased.
"Simon, you are like a rock;
You are such a loyal friend to me!
Like the rock, you will remain firm in you faith that I am King of
the Lions.
No longer shall you be called Simple Simon.
Henceforth you shall be called Rocky."

11 Rocky grinned.

12 "But Rocky, my friend", Leo continued,
"The day will come that you will deny me!"

13 Groaned Rocky, "No master, I shall never deny you!"

14 "Indeed Rocky", replied Leo,
"After denying me twice, the rooster will crow three times."

15 "Cockadoodledoo!", came the sound from above.

16 "The rooster!", moaned Rocky.

17 "Three times!", Leo roared.

18 "Cockadoodledoo Cockadoodledoo!"

19 "The rooster?"

20 "Three times!"

21 "Cockadoodledoo!"

22 "Oh!"

V

1 Leo went on to work great wonders among the lions.

2 Leo walked with Marlene and saw a big party going on.
Two lions were getting married,
But there was no wine at the wedding, only water.
Leo roared to the moon
And the water changed to wine.
Leo saved the best wine for last.
Everybody had a good time and without getting drunk.

3 Leo climbed to the top of Mount Victoria to fast.
He became hungry.
Along came a weasel that tempted Leo.
He said, "Command these stones that they be made bread!
Did you not say, "If your son asks for bread, do you give him a stone?"

4 Leo growled, "Even monkeys don't live by banana,
But by every word that proceeds from Diana."

5 The weasel tried other tactics.
He challenged Leo, "If you are King of the Lions,
Jump off the cliff
And the Pegasus will save you!"

6 Leo replied, "Diana can't be tested
Or my rump will be arrested!"

7 The weasel squealed, "I will give you all in the world if you worship me!"

8 Leo replied, "Get thee hence, Satyr!
I must serve only Diana!"

9 Leo and his friends had a lot of fun playing games on the beach of the Indian Ocean.
Leo walked on the surface of the surf and roared,
"Let me see you do this!"

10 Rocky tried to walk on the water,
But one hundred tail lengths out,
He saw waves coming,
Was frightened
And started to sink.
Leo pulled him out just in time to keep him from drowning.

11 Leo went about healing all diseases
Simply by calling out the name, Diana.

12 Ten leopards played in the trees.
A branch broke,
And they fell into a mud puddle.
They were so dirty,
It was impossible to see their spots.
No matter how they tried,
They couldn't shake off the dirt.

13 They approached Leo and roared:
"Canst thou make us whole
And make clean the leopard soul?"

14 Leo replied, "In the Congo River jump
And all thine dirt there dump!"

15 The leopards were cleansed,
But only one returned to give Leo thanks.

16 Leo roared, "Where are the other nine:
All clean white lambs of mine?
Only one still can be seen.
Go now, be forever clean!"

17 A jackal approached Leo and begged:
"I implore thee for help;
Come heal my whelp!"

18 Leo growled, "As we cannot fashion garments out of logs,
We cannot give things holy unto the dogs!"

19 The jackal pleaded, "When lions have finished their master sums,
The dogs come along and nibble the crumbs."

20 Leo roared with delight:
"Tis very brilliant and true what she saith;
Among lions I never have seen so much faith.
Go hurry now back to your little one soon.
You will find he is healed by the light of the moon."

VI

1 Leo saw lions gathered around a fair lioness, snarling and clawing at her.
He enquired what the commotion was about.

2 They roared, "She is an adulteress.
Every season she mates with a different cat!"

3 Leo roared, "Settle back and be polite;
The one without sin
May now move in;
He is the one who should take the first bite."

4 None moved.

5 Leo roared, "I proclaim she is all right,
For I, the sinless, will not bite!"

6 The other lions dispersed.

7 Leo approached and learned her name was Maggie.

8 "Why do you weep, my beautiful kitty?", he asked.

9 "Oh Lord, I am a bad pussy;
Every season I mate with a different cat!"

10 "My dear Maggie," Leo growled softly.
"The moon will save you;
The moon will take away your sins;
Whenever the moon is above;
You must be naked and expose beneath it.
If you avoid the grass
You will not be covered.
Then you will be purified
And you will sin no more!"

11 Maggie did as he said
And ran out naked
Whenever the moon was above.
Henceforth, she remained faithful to one mate.
Monkeys spread the rumor that the mate was Leo,
But nobody knows for sure.
The elephants never forget
But think this is too sordid to discuss.
We do know that the pussy stayed faithful to one mate.

VII

1 Leo was fond of a lioness named Judy.
He liked to romp with her on the plains.

2 Leo did not always get along with Judy.
They wrestled together
and she tried to inflict pain with a sharp bite.

3 She growled, "What do you mean, we shouldn't kill?
Without my meat I am sure to get ill!"

4 One day Leo growled, "You know how others are trying to slay
me.
One of these days now, you will betray me!"

5 Judy retorted, "Why should I, such foolishness makes me swoon!"

6 Roared Leo, "I'm reading the face of the moon:
She says the deed dirty is meant just for Judy,
So please hustle off now and function your duty!"

VIII

(Aleph)
1 Not all lions accepted what Leo preached,
But he roared his ideas to them
Whenever they gathered together.

2 He spoke again unto the other lions:
"You must love the moon.
Whenever the moon is above,
You must be naked and exposed beneath it.
Avoid the grass and you will not be covered;
Then the moon will grant you whatever you desire."

3 The other lions roared with anger:
"The king of the beasts must be decently covered.
We must not subject ourselves to such lewd exposure, especially
beneath Diana.

4 Catapus, Anna and others started after Leo.
Leo hid in the bushes with Rocky.

5 Lions searched around the bushes, demanding, "Where is Leo?"

6 Judy went over to Leo and gave him a kiss.
Lions surrounded Leo.
Rocky leaped on Catapus and bit off his ear.

7 Leo growled, "Because we must obey the laws,
Even sharks can't live by jaws."

8 He looked up at the moon and let out a roar.
The ear of Catapus was restored whole like the other.

9 Lions turned on Leo
And drove him from the grassland toward the woodland country.
Leo bid Rocky to come with him.
Leo was driven into the forest.
Rocky leaped into the forest with his friend, Leo.
There they were surrounded by angry wolves.

10 "So you are King of the Lions?", they growled.

11 "Indeed I am!", answered Leo bravely.

(Beth)
12   The wolves approached Rocky.
"Do you know this cat?", they growled.

13 "No, I know him not!", he answered.

14 "Do you know this cat?", they growled again.

15 "No, I know him not!", he repeated.

16 A rooster meanwhile flew overhead and landed on a branch of a
tree. "Cockadoodledoo! Cockadoodledoo! Cockadoodledoo!"

17 Rocky slunk to the grassland in shame, his tail between his
legs.

(Gimel)
18 Catapus said to Judy, "Why the glum look on your face?
Here is a nice bone that we promise you!"

19 Judy dropped the bone and slunk toward the high cliffs.
She jumped off the cliff
And her body was dashed to pieces on the rocks below.

IX

1 The wolves turned toward Leo and demanded;
"Hey you with the mane like Davy's star!
Who do you think you are?
Are you a superstar?
We give you one hour to get out of the jungle
And back to the grassland where you belong."

2 Angry lions continued to roar:
"We did not ask him to be king!"

3 They blocked Leo's way,
So he could not return to the grassland.

4 The wolves were very rude;
They turned on Leo and chewed
Till his corpse was the tiniest pieces
And left then to rot in his feces.
There he was left as dead;
A mile away was his head,
And roses began to bud
From the ground that was soaked with his blood.

5 But Leo was the toughest lion ever;
He had bile of every color in his liver;
He expected extinction never.
Leo recovered in only three days,
Lifted by Diana's warm and loving rays.

X

(Aleph)
1 Leo sauntered back to the grassland.
The first he met was Maggie.

2 Maggie was delighted.
She roared, "Oh Lord,
I heard it said
That you were dead,
But I love you so much
I could still feel your touch,
So I could tell
That you were well!"

3 She snuggled up to him and gave him a big kiss.

(Beth)
4 Then he came upon Rocky and the kibitzer Tommy.

5 Tommy thought he was rather clever
And frequently made fun of his retarded friend, Rocky.

6 "Oh Tom, O cat!", moaned Rocky,
"I denied my master twice;
The cock crowed three times.
I am nothing but a chicken!"

7 "Better to be a live chicken than a dead lion, Rockhead!"

8 Along came Leo.

9 "What are you doing in these parts, Stranger?", growled Tom and
Rocky.

10 Do you remember me not? I am Leo, King of the Lions!"

11 "Master!", roared Rocky with delight.

12 "Baloney!", roared Tom.

13 "Do you remember me not?", asked Leo.

14 "You are only a ghost!", snorted Tom.

15 "See these tooth and nail marks!", growled Leo patiently.

16 Flabbergasted, Tom roared:
"You are King of the Lions!
You are King of the Lions!"

XI

1 Leo climbed to the top of Mr. Victoria.

2 Every day, when the moon rose, he roared, "Diana, Diana!"

3 Then lo! A miracle! The moon began to shine brighter.

4 Then a loud growl...
And screeches, roars, bays, yelps
And every animal could understand every other animal's
Yelps, bays, roars, screeches and howl.

XII

1 Salamander was a religious fanatic
He put no phylacteries away in the attic.
He had a mate but would copulate
With her only once each season. ˙
But lo, Diana smiled on Sal;
His lioness had one cub every season.

2 Sal loved Diana;
He thought her a prize;
Every day, he waited for Diana to rise.

3 Whenever he had the power
He roared every day for an hour:
"Blessed; be Diana, Queen of the Universe;
If I am good, then you are good, and then you can't get worse!
Yah! Yah! Yah!
Ani tov ata tov lo rah!"
And still he continued to croon,
"Hear O lions, our moon Diana is one moon!"

4 Sal quarreled bitterly with all the friends of Leo, growling:
"Wash your paws and mane at least,
If you have any virtue as a kingly beast!"

5 Only one named Steve dared argue with Sal,
Growling, "Off in constant sin you go,
Rejecting your prophets, especially Leo."

6 Sal leaped on Steve and chewed him to pieces
And made it all kosher by salting his feces.
He hexed the others with pins in the head
And saved the blood for his Passover bread.

7 Sal stalked off into the woodland country
And set about to conspire with the wolves.

8 Sal roared, "You see all those lions rejoicing,
Their praises to Leo are voicing.
All night they continue to sing:
'Under Leo, we all can be king!'
If friends of Leo you kill,
Then lions can work no more ill!"

9 Joyfully the wolves howled:
"On Sal the wolf depends.
Hey, point us Leo's friends!"

10 The wolves prepared to make excursions into the grassland
And kill all of Leo's friends.

XIII

1 Communing with Diana was Leo;
He knew all that went on the lands below.
He came down from Mt. Victoria.
He took the side of a fat antelope.
Leo had such great surgical skill
That the antelope pranced off unhurt.

2 He marched through the grassland and met upon Sal,
Who was scouting for victims for wolves.
Leo cornered Sal at a cliff.
Sal was scared, thinking how rough and tough Leo must be
To have come back after being attacked by so many wolves.

3 Then lo and behold:
Leo in friendship held out his paw
As if Sal was his brother or father or mother or cousin in law.
"I forgive you for fighting with my friends and even
Forgive you for good for the murder of Steven!"

4 Sal nervously took Leo's paw in his own
And remarked how in noble stature Leo had grown.
Leo smiled warmly at Sal and kissed him cheekly;
"You are King of the Lions", confessed Sal meekly.

5 They sat and dined on the antelope's side,
knowing they were the lambs and the ewe was the bride.
Then for several hours they rapped,
And Leo could tell that something had snapped.

6 He roared: "No more are you called Sal,
For you are my pal;
I call you Pal!"

7 Then Leo roared, "Lo, the moon
Is coming nigh soon!"

8 Pal looked up at the moon.
It was full and especially bright.
It scorched the retina of Pal's eyes and left him blind.

XIV

1 Pal staggered about groping with his paws,
Hoping to get help
Before a jackal would bother him.
He chanced upon Rocky.

2 Rocky was startled by the change in the countenance of Sal, now
Pal.
Beside Pal's blindness, Rocky detected a new humility.
Not a sound was exchanged,
But they immediately understood each other.
The moon smiled on them.

3 Rocky immediately forgave Pal.
He remembered what Leo had taught him:
"Love your enemies."
Rocky had never stopped loving Sal,
Even when Sal was hateful.
Rocky licked Pal's eyes
And Pal's sight was restored.
From them on, Rocky and Pal were loving friends.

4 Pal was brighter than Rocky and took the lead.
He growled, "We go all over the world
And tell all animals the good news about Leo.
All animals will be brothers!
Peace on Earth!
Good will to all beasts!"

5 Both set out.

6 Pal traveled far and wide to distant lands, converting all the
other animals.
Even Asian tigers,
Australian kangaroos,
North American cougars
And South American Jaguars all heard the good news of the
wonderful teaching of Leo, King of the Lions.

7 Pal roared to all animals:
"Set affection not on Earth but on the moon above,
For she's the one with whom we strive to be at one in love,
And when Leo will appear, we all appear with him in glory,
So gather now and listen; be acquainted with his story!"

8 The hippos in the swampland bayed at the sky even with no moon
above.
They made a big racket.

9 They grunted, "Give praise to the unknown moon!
We pray that our music is getting in tune!
Then the time will come that we find full salvation
All over and under throughout every nation!"

10 Pal roared, "Her that you ignorantly worship, now I declare!
She goes through her phases and lo, she is there.
She is the one who shines nightly above
And all of us animals witness her love!"

11 Lions were very angry,
Because Pal accepted other animals,
Even those whose sexual organs were not bitten short,
As was customary among lions.

12 Pal roared at them:
"Your virtue as king of the beasts is gone
So the ends of your peckers are put back on!"

13 Lions roamed into the swampland and roared to the hippos:
"Pal must be bitten into saw dust;
He tells you Leo is your king, not August!"

14 Hippos joined lions and chewed Pal to pieces.
A river then carried off Pal with his feces,
But as soon as Diana appeared overhead,
Then pal strutted off and then roared, "I'm not dead!"

15 A hippopotamus with a defective leg limped toward Pal.
Pal let out a roar to the moon.

16 The hippopotamus walked straight to the other hippos, Grunting,
"Pal hath made me straight!
Now in praise let's cease our hate!"

17 Then Pal healed all animals that came to him, just by calling
out the name, Diana.

18 Some hippos were under the spell of weasels,
Who made the hippos upset by biting them,
Causing flowers to squirt in their faces
And pulling other practical jokes.

19 Some lions came along
Who hoped to be provided food for their services.
They roared at the weasels:
"We admonish you weasels to stay out of reach
In the name of Leo, whom Pal doth preach!"

20 The weasels squealed, "We all know Leo and Pal very well,
But you lions turn even us off with you smell!"

21 The weasels leaped on those lions and chewed them to pieces,
Making them all eat the words in their thesis,
Although all the words smelled s bad as their feces.

22 The hippos all praised the name of Leo.

23 Then Pal went back to the African Grassland.
He knew that trouble awaited him there,
But the moon smiled on Pal.
Pal felt that Diana ordered him to go.

24 He roared at the other lions, "In the grasslands you cannot in comfort stay
If your king you will not follow and obey!"

25 They roared, "Leave us alone with our Passover feasts!
We are all the kings of the beasts!"

26 They set upon Pal
And chewed and clawed at him
And he just barely escaped.

XV

1 The travels of Rocky were far more limited.
The poor dolt marched right into woodland country
To preach unto the wolves and other vicious predators.

2 Some wolves growled:
"Behold that lion;
He is surely lyin'
How dare he let out a peep
An disturb our sleep!

3 "We wolves are the kings of the beasts;
We march to the Souths and the Norths and the Wests and the Easts.
We defeated elephants climbing our hills--
This proves no one can question our skills!

4 We are king as much as that arrogant rabble
How dare they let out a babble
Or gaggle
Or swaggle
Or cackle?"

5 Yelling boos and hisses,
They set upon Rocky and chewed him to pieces;
The result was left there to phthisis;
I have already said what to do with his feces.

6 But brothers, even the wolf has a conscience.

7 Some growled, "That was not a nice thing to do to Rocky.
He does not claim to be king of the beasts.
He says it matters not whether you be a lion or hippopotamus.
Leo is king of all the animals.
We wolves did not kill Leo;
The lions refused to let him back in.
Let us follow Leo,
And the moon will grant us all we desire!"

8 They showered great honor on the remains of Rocky
And called him Poppa.
They buried him with their own great leaders.

XVI

1 In wolf society, the term Poppa was a great honor.
Nobody calls his mother's mate Poppa.
Nobody knew who he was,
Because no she-wolf ever said no to a male.
A bitch like that needs not even be asked.

2 Community chiefs all marched to a large clearing in the woods.
By a large majority, they elected a second Poppa,
Announcing, "Avemus Poppa!"

3 The new Poppa growled:
"To avoid the weasel's hex
We all follow Leo Rex
Sic semper gloria
Be-a his storia
Whose chvrch to Diana erex."

4 Unfortunately it took thousands of years for those wolves to
really follow Leo,
Because it was hard to start following Leo instead of their own
Poppa.

5 Under orders from the Poppa, wolves continued to kill lions for
many years, growling,
"They were the ones who murdered our king,
So as Cosa Nostra, we do our thing!"

6 They drove them from the African grasslands
And scattered them all over the world.

7 Other animals followed the Poppa, all called Poppists,
Including all the frogs, united under King Charleybog.

8 A camel named Hammy went about preaching.
He was mocked by Leonians,
"Before you even start to talk,
Please correct you awkward walk!"

9 They drove him into the desert.

10 Fortunately, he could walk many miles without water.
He trudged all over the world, bleating to all the animals:
"Whenever to the moon we holler,
Respectfully we call, 'Dialla',
That name we humbly say,
When we bow to her five times per day."

11 The tigers took to Hammy like ducks take to water.
They were sick of the hypocrisy of the wolves:
The wolves claimed to follow Leo,
But continued to prey on smaller and weaker animals.

12 A Poppa decided to fight with some tigers for holy land
And thousands of wolves set out as one band
To the land where Leo and Rocky first met,
But where tigers converted by Hammy were set.
A nation of Hammy existed by laws
Letting tigers make maximum use of their jaws.

13 "If an animal fighting for Hammy should die,
In Dialla's bosom forever will lie!"

14 On the way, the wolves set on lions and chewed them to pieces;
On the trail to the East was left only their feces.
But the tigers were tougher than wolves and were able to hold their
own;
They forced the wolves back without needing to throw a stone.

15 In those days, kings and other leaders owned most of the land and had special privileges.
Most others had to give up all ambitions in deference to Leo.
Some contributed to impoverished animals.

16 Only lions were considered entitled to grub all they desired.
As descendants of their great patriarch, Abe,
They were all kings.
They did not have to follow Leo.
Many other animals wanted more for themselves
And joined with the lions.
They began to look and roar like lions,
Even ones not descended from Abe.

17 Lions roared louder than any other animals.
Many believed them when they claimed
That they were more charitable than followers of Leo,
Even though they aided mostly their own kind and others that joined them.

XVII

(Aleph)
1 A cheetah named Martin grew up longing to serve the Poppa.
He joined the Poppa's community.
But he was dismayed by the bad things going on there.

2 Martin growled at the Poppa, "What is the inquisition for?
We animals should kill no more!
Your bishops are getting out of hand;
From corner to corner they rape the land."

3 The Poppa retorted, "Get away from me, will you?
Or I'll have my wolf pack kill you!"

4 Martin told others that there should be no Poppa.

5 "Listen and I will tell you about Leo.
Leo says, 'love the moon with all your heart and soul and mind--
That's what you must do first to unwind.
Love other animals as you love the moon and the moon loves you!
That is all you ever have to do.'
That is all you need to know;
Don't listen to your Mamma and Poppa;
Get gold for your copper;
In Leo you must grow!"

6 This made the Poppa very angry.
He ordered that Martin be killed,
But no wolf was fast enough to catch and kill the cheetah, Martin,
Who was soon protected by his own followers.
The wolves went on a diet,
Eating only worms,
To show their loyalty to their Poppa.

7 The Poppa sent bulls all over the world to warn all animals,
Snorting, "Martin is covered with lice;
His words are preposterous
Like a charging rhinosterous;
He is getting fat
And not only that,
None of the things that he tells you are nice!"

(Beth)
8 One bull said, "To Leo and his friends belong great reverence
Which we must bestow them without severance:
Great Poppas and Poppists we must please;
We must go down on our knees;
We must kneel
And call out the names of those animals great
Who leave all others second rate,
And sins they forgive and diseases they heal,
Though only one moon, Diana, we worship;
To have any other moon is a curseship!"

9 Early wolves worshipped many planets and moons.
It was hard for the Poppas to change that too much.

10 Their cubs worshipped a fat old fairy, dragged around by a
team of reindeer.
They expected presents from him during the twelfth moon of every
year, thinking they were celebrating the day Leo was born.
Giraffes have long necks and even longer memories but refuse to
tell anybody what day Leo was born,
But wolves couldn't stop having orgies a week before the new year
as did their ancient ancestors.

11 Later, Poppists and Martinists killed each other for thirty
years,
Even though they all claimed to love all others
Because they followed Leo.
Many frogs who wanted to follow Martin were massacred at St.
Bartholowmeow.

XVIII

1 Listen to this bull!
"If an animal takes a mate,
He may not take another one until death.
Cast out no mate no matter what kind of rat she is,
Even if stuck with a porcupine."

2 The rats were insulted,
But most of them continued to love and support the Poppa.
It is a race that has to be chaste;
The cats chase them.

3 "Animals must strive to have a cub every time they copulate.
Females who do not so strive,
Are sure to go to the pots
Or down to the loops.

4 "If a female destroys her cub before birth,
She must be avoided by all other animals
And she is sure to be damned by the beavers and go to the herring.

5 "Females must keep covered
When animals get together under Diana;
They may take no positions of leadership, especially at that time.

6 Other animals heard this bull and were annoyed,
So another bull went out that bellowed,
"Animals no longer have to go to the sea for meat on the sixth day
every week.
They may go whenever they please,
Because beavers do not build dams there.

7 "Animals no longer have to bark like the ancient wolves,
Whenever they get together under Diana.
They may continue with their natural chatter
Without being dammed by any beavers
Or going to herring."

8 This made animals less afraid,
So they began to cautiously approach the Poppa,
Knowing they could do so
Without being dammed by beavers
Or going to herring.

9 The hyenas thought it was funny and kept laughing.

10 The ostriches did not give a dam and kept their heads in the sand.

11 The opossums just played dead.

XIX

1 Many years ago the foxes were subject to a tyrannical king named John.
He had a violent temper.
He hired wolves to fight against rams in the hills, frogs and other enemies.
Other foxes were reluctant to serve him,
As John believed that he could confine any subject who displeased him.

2 John's nephew, Arty, approached John's den insisting:
"With you sir, I pick a bone
Because I am the rightful heir to the throne."

3 John's chased him off with his sharp teeth.

4 John even defied the Poppa,
Who was considered boss by many animals.
A wolf arrived as ambassador
To recommend a bishop for the foxes.

5 John barked, "Don't serve such a dish up;
I accept not this bishop!
Let the king alone rule!
Be off now, you fool!"

6 The wolf who reigned as Poppa growled:
"John makes me so harried,
Let none there be married!
My curse on his head,
We will bury no dead!
Fox priests there procure
No more food for the poor!
Now let every fox pout
Till the bum is kicked out!"

7 Many foxes starved.
There was a great clamor against John
Until he bowed before the Poppa and made peace.

8 Arty's body was found under a cliff.
Foxes accused John, growling,
"You make us a problem too tough to use logs.
We will send no more meat to get wolves to fight frogs!"
.

9 John marched off to the top of the highest hill with the leaders
of the rebellion.
He left a paw print there, signifying that he would respect
individual rights and limit the power of the throne.
All disputes would be settled by juries of animals selected from
the general public.
The paw print remained there by the eagles nests, signifying
freedom.

10 Foxes battled with frogs for a hundred years.
A female named Joan heard voices from Diana telling her:
"You must lead the army of frogs.
Gather them together out of the bogs!"
The frogs fought valiantly but Joan was captured.
The foxes roasted her and enjoyed frogs legs for dinner.

11 King Henry did not want to be stuck with the same vixen until
death,
Disobeying bulls sent by the Poppa.
Others foxes agreed that they would support King Henry,
Even if he broke with the Poppa.
King Henry barked, "To the Defender of the Faith all hark,
Because the way that Leo roars, I bark!"
He bit off the heads of a few dissenters.

12 One mate complained,
"We must reform before it is too late,
Because no beast should stray for a different mate!"
Henry, displeased by what she said,
Quickly proceeded to bite off her head.
King Henry had six mates before he was through.

13 King Charlie confiscated land and other property from his subjects,
Without letting a jury hear the case
According to King John's covenant.

14 Charlie barked, "I rule by lunar right,
For the king is perfect in Diana's sight!"

15 Foxes grabbed him and bit his head off.
Prime Minister Oliver ruled as Lord Protector,
While foxes were left without a king.
Oliver sent cohorts to capture Charlie's children,
So that the monarchy could not be restored.
Charlie Jr. could not be found;
He was hiding in a tree,
Nobody bothered him as he looked like a squirrel.

16 After many years, Oliver was through
And Charlie returned to be crowned king.

17 Even after the monarchy was restored,
The rule over the foxes became more and more liberal,
Because kings remembered what happened to Charlie,
But foxes continued to lord it over cougars and other animals across the seas.
They growled in unison:
"You chaps will have to accept our sire,
Because Diana never sets on the fox empire!"

18 Mice on a nearby island rebelled.
Many including Patrick, Sean and Mickey Mouse starved themselves to death.
Animals all over the world were outraged until mice were granted freedom.

19 Growling of the cougars became more and more angry:
"No king can take of our meat by taxation,
Unless foxes give us full representation!
Over our continent will be defendants:
The cougars now declare independence!"

20 One animal in North America was a beaver named George who famous for honesty.
Once, when he was young, he confessed immediately when he had gnawed down his father's cherry tree.

21 Cougars rallied around George to start fighting for independence.
But the war started badly:
A winter was cold
And many froze to death while marching with George.

22 Foxes became overconfident;
They thought they had things completely under control,
Especially with the help of wolves serving as mercenaries.

23 Cougars crept South for a whole year.
At year's end, the pack of wolves relaxed, celebrating Leo's birthday.
George and his band quietly swam across a river,
Crept upon those wolves and slaughtered them.
Cougars kept jumping on foxes from hills and tree tops
Until the foxes surrendered.

24 Cougars gathered to prepare a new constitution.
It provided for a Grand Cougar and Vicious Cougar but no king.
All animals should be allowed to speak and worship as they please
Because all animals are equal.
Any North American animal could rise to become Grand Cougar.

25 George became the first Grand Cougar.
He moved into a white birch tree.

26 Even without a king, the cougar's government became more tyrannical than that of the foxes,
Especially after George was gone.
Animals were discouraged from voting,
Especially black panthers and others held in low esteem.
For many years, cougars kept black panthers as slaves.
They had to stay in fields, picking cotton to keep cougars warm in the winter
And given little to wear in return.

27 Northern Cougars freed the few black panthers among themselves,
and objected to slavery in the South.
One avid proponent of freedom was named Abe.
Abe was elected Grand Cougar,
Getting the most votes among four candidates.

28 Southern cougars were dismayed.
They separated and formed their own Government.
This made Abe growl with rage
And he resolved to reunite North America by force, if necessary.
A bloody war started.

29 In an early battle, Northern cougars were horrified
To see a bull run and trample all over them.
Their general Ulysses growled,
"Though this conflict seems a bummer,
We will fight it on this line if it takes all Summer!"
The Northern cougars finally prevailed.
The cougars were reunited.
The black panthers were freed.

30 No cougar, even Abe, thought that black panthers were equal.
Krazy Kat Krusaders marched, calling them 'coons'.
They hung flaming wolf teeth in front of dens of black panthers and
their sympathizers to warn them:
"If high in society, you think you can go,
We will do to you, boy, what we did to Leo!"

31 Red deer were treated even worse,
Even though they were the first animals ever in North America.
Land was stolen from them and promises were broken.
Many red deer were killed,
When they went on the warpath bleating,
"Scalp-up pale panther!"

XX

1 In other lands, animals were hardly better off without a king.

2 Hungry frogs mobbed around the royal lily pad and demanded:
"Tell us no lies;
We want more flies!"

3 Queen Toni laughed and replied:
"I'm really at a loss for words;
If they have no flies, let them eat birds!
What do they want avec moi?
Throw them in the cesspool, un, deux, trois!"

4 Frogs invaded a lily pad where many were held captive, freeing the prisoners.
Many descended on the king and queen.
Frogs dragged King Louis and Queen Toni to the middle of a pond
Where their heads were snapped off by a big turtle.

5 The new leaders suspected that some frogs conspired with wolves and foxes to restore the monarchy.
They ordered heads snapped off on the slightest suspicion.
This alarmed the population,
And a radical leader was dragged to the snapping turtle.

6 Another leader was taking a bath in his private water hole.
He invited a female over to wash him.
She stabbed him to death with a sharp branch.

7 A general named Nap took over and restored order.
He set up a code of law for all animals to follow.

8 The Poppa was called to crown him emperor.
Nap grabbed the crown of brambles away from the Poppa and
croaked:
"I made myself emperor, not the Pop.
I dance on the lily pads; he goes wop!
I tell it as it is while he has to fib it.
Rib-bit, Rib-bit!"

9 Nap had megalomanic ideas about who he was.
He thought he could liberate all animals from oppressive
monarchies, enlisting wolves, cheetahs, eagles and other powerful
beasts.
He took over many lands.

10 Finally, the frogs invaded the land where the bears lived.
The bears hardly had to fight,
Because it was so cold there
That many frogs froze to death.

11 After Nap was defeated,
The frogs restored the reign of the kings
And called for a brother of the last king.

12 One time, Nap returned from the island where he was exiled,
But foxes and wolves closed in on him again.

13 Nap croaked, "If my army of frogs doesn't know what to do,
You can call my water hole Waterloo!"
So many big and strong frogs perished in Nap's wars
That most frogs are small and weak to this day.

14 Bears later disposed of their king,
But nobody noticed the difference in their land.
Leadership was restricted to party members.
Deer and other weaker animals were refused independence they demanded
And were brutally exploited by the bears.
They were expected to eat the same things that the bears ate
But were given inferior honey.
All animals under their rule were forced to go to sleep early every night,
So they could not see Diana.

15 To the West were some kodiak grizzly bears.
They wanted to restore the king to the throne.
They welcomed invading wolves with friendly bear hugs.
They learned much from the wolves about how to keep domestic order.

16 After the war, kodiak grizzly bears served at most posts of the bears' secret police.
They set up a tyrannical system over all lands controlled by the bears.
Neighbors informed on each other
And whelp squealed on their parents.
Animals were afraid to speak freely,
Afraid that a kodiak grizzly bear (K.G.B.) might be listening.

XXI

1 On top of Mount Victoria, Leo kept roaring,

2 "Diana, Diana", when the moon came up soaring,

3 And lo, the moon, it shone then more bright,

4 And other miracle, a sightly delight;

5 It never fails;

6 Many rabbits, deer and other herbivores, especially asses developed very round and broad rumps and tails,

7 And What was more weird,

8 From those rumps, especially rumps of asses, nerve cells completely disappeared.

9 Any animal that desired meat could jump

10 And bite off a piece of another's rump,

11 Causing no pain

12 And hunger would no longer remain,

13 And it came to pass

14 That life became like a game of tag, especially when they all began to grab a piece of the ass.

15 Will the squirrels think I'm a nut who just has to rave

16 If I say many animals continued to misbehave?

XXII
(Aleph)
1 Once there was a wolf;
His name was Doolf,
Then changed to Dolf.
He barked, "walf, walf!"
And was a fright
And was the true light.

2 He howled, "I am Aries, the ram;
I butt in wherever I can;
I am that I am!"

3 He stood like a candle on top of a hill
And no one could ever dare counter her will.
His angry jowls foamed
For some lions had roamed
With their families and goods
And settled in the woods.

4 In their dens they wallowed;
Some of them followed
The words of Leo; some did not;
Some smoked pot.

5 Some let their manes grow till they looked like King Kong
Or had a piece chopped from the end of their schlong.

6 Some ate matzah;
Mixed with grass, it's called potzah.
Their mamas cooked chicken soup;
They were quite a group.

7 Many were prosperous
From the Rhine to the Bosporus,
At business were shrewd,
Causing wolves there to brood,
So Dolf looked upon them with envious eyes
And disdaining their virtues, he poured out his lies.

8 So low were they rated,
The fearer hated
Every lion with a cold passion.
He had lost his ration.

9 Early one morning, Dolf arose and put on his togs
And he called together the other dogs.

10 Das ist was der Deutcher sung:
"Achtung!"

11 "Behold dose lions
Und Roarin's und kryin's;
Vy should dey be better
Mit ears dat are vetter
In any veather?"

12 "Ve volves must look after our own
Or be left mitout efen ein bone!
Our own, you know, are kaptured by bears to der East,
Bear led by lions who don't belief in money
But diefin' lions dere schteal all der honey!"

13 "Der volf ist only ein beast,
But ein ficious beast!
Zince der blut must kontinue to schpill,
Der beast has der duty to kill!
Now sil fous plait, more of mein schvill!

14 "Ich kare, you kare
Und bevare
Of Leo's teachinks
Und krazy preachinks!
Do deserff ein schoff
If der dangerous
Out-of-rangerous
Leo gets you to loff,
To loff eferybody efen der lion
No matter how tryin'"

15   Dolf continued to sing:
"Another thing:
Leo ist ein Lion, und ve hate lions
Und deir zinginks of Zions!

16 "You von't be bored
If you zee how de lions hoard
All of de fattest karkasses,
Like Noah used to hoard
Into ein zoggy ark asses.
Ve volves are left to schtarff und left mit keiner!
Dere vas nefer ein howdy doo finer!

17 "Ve vere plagued mit lion und locust
Zince first ein feline her beau kissed!
Ve haf much to komplain about:
Ve haf nothin' to eat but kraut!"

18 "So on, let's do as ve must;
In Dolf you dogs all must trust!
Ve march to herring und back
In kourage, ve volves nefer lack!"

(Beth)
19 Then the loud thundrin' sound
Came 'round very loud: "Heil Dolf!"
Bayed the wolves as a pack there, "Walf, walf, ralph, malph!"

20 No more yappin's or cryin's,
The wolves set on the lions
And chewed them to pieces.
Even Fritz
Did it in Auschwitz;
No one could see
Through the Zyclon B.

21 Don't call me facetious;
They buried Cohen's feces
But some had scarred faces;
After being raped,
A few escaped;
A few could survive;
They were still alive;
They joined with others
And called them brothers
In their homes
And under domes
In the grasslands and other places.

(Gimel)
22 Wolves under the command of Dolf made war against many
other animals,
Because Dolf wanted to rid the whole world of lions.

23 Nearby, a big moose stormed into a land inhabited by guinea
pigs.
He bellowed: "To resist me, there is no use;
Now I take over as Il Duce!"

24 He ordered guinea pigs to march into North Africa,
To take over land belonging to baboons,
He stomped around
And trampled on any guinea pigs that did not obey him.

25 The king of the baboons called himself, the Lion of Judea.
Under his command, they gave the guinea pigs a tough fight.
The moose bellowed:
This dance is too difficult for us to jig;
As even baboons beat the guinea pig!

The moose begged Dolf for help.
Wolves sent by Dolf enabled the moose to triumph.

26 There were nasty sharks off the coast of Asia
Who joined the alliance with the moose and Dolf.

27 Dolf cast his eyes on other lands, growling,
"All of the volves must march as one band
So ve rule where dere are volves in any land!"

28 The wolves marched and easily took over some land belonging
to some polecats in the East.
Next to fall were Amsterdam, Rotterdam and other dams belonging
to beavers.
As result of the broken dams, the wolves chewed up the frogs with
ease.

29 They came upon foxes protecting the frogs.
The foxes had to get across the channel to their own country in a
hurry.
There were friendly dolphins who were no relatives of Dolf..
They carried the foxes to safety.
Dolf sent woodpeckers to demolish the forests inhabited by foxes.
They were hindered by tough resistance by English sparrows.

30 The fox leader, named Winston, barked:
"We've been chasing rabbits for many years;
Now we must survive by blood, sweat and tears!"

31 Meanwhile one species had cause to gloat,
For at peace and independent stayed the mountain goat.

32 Finally, wolves invaded the land where the bears lived,
While the weather got colder and colder.
The wolves could not find a soul among their enemy.
The bears were all hibernating.

33 Many wolves froze to death
And other animals closed in on them.
Even clams assisted in shelling them!

34 Sharks and beetles took over one Pacific island after another.
Sharks chewed up many cougars swimming off their vacation island.
The cougars had to think of a way to stop the sharks.
They dug up some dinosaurs, believed extinct,
But well preserved beneath the ground.

35 The Grand Cougar in North America, named Harry, growled:
"I cannot wish my enemies well;
Let's send a dinosaur to give them hell!"

36 The cougars unleashed Godzilla,
Who devastated two schools of sharks.
That forced the sharks to surrender.

(Daleth)

37 The wolves were defeated by cougars and foxes and bears
With some help from the frogs
Who divided the land that belonged to the dogs.

38 And from camels were heard then loud painful bleats,
For some lions considered them tasty for eats.
The bears gave the camels their full support,
But against the cougars could not hold the fort.
The cougars supported their cousinish cat;
In the grasslands, the lions could stay and get fat.

39 The camels attracted only a smile
From the face of the treacherous crocodile,
And later, the camels continued to boil
For a tiger named EXXON owned all the oil.

XXIII

1 Some opossums believed that Diana predicted the future for them
and began to moan as follows:
"Call the moon nothing but Diana!
Aren't there other moons beside Diana?
We must not confuse them with Diana!"

2 These animals were called Diana's Gigolows.

3 Whenever there were wars and other world conflicts, they just
hung by the branches or stayed in bed
Or just played dead.

4 They moaned, "We must wait until Diana tells us to fight;
Only she is always right!"

5 They protected themselves with this verb,
"Do not disturb!"

6 Though they disturbed all other creatures,
Howling out now and then
At entrances to every den;
They thought they were Diana's teachers
But were called "Diana's nuisances
With fit-just-for-a-zoo senses."

7 Since gigolows always stayed in bed,
Hung by their tails or just played dead,
Except when others they disturbed,
Yapping out Diana's word,
Whenever lying in the mud,
They wanted none to touch their blood,
Even if one's whelp was crying,
In agonizing pain was crying.

8 And it came to pass as follows:
Other animals became very mad,
Thinking Diana's Gigolows were bad
And they frequently drove away the Gigolows.

XXIV

1 All over the forest this news was heard;
A marmot named Joe had discovered the word,
Written plainly in tablets of gold,
All of the news from the world of old:

2 "Once when Leo in person appeared
Unto the cougars his starry head reared,
Saying, "just like a few lions of old
Males may take more than one mate in their fold."

3 Many animals altered their lives:
Some of the males took many wives.
Marmot varmints had to go
When cougars grabbed and murdered Joe.

4 Cougars kept driving marmots West;
They thought every one of them was a pest.
Marmots went to their desert
And there began to hurt.

5 Finally marmots repented:
From polygamy relented,
But not from every sin.
They accepted all others
And called them brothers,
But it took one hundred years
(They disliked dark ears)
Before they let black panthers in.

XXV

1 Once upon a time there was a cougar named Millie
Who was considered very silly
She joined a strange alliance:
Following Leo was made a science.

2 She was injured once when she fell from a tree;
She growled to the moon and she quickly was free.

3 Growled Millie, "I hope you won't swoon
When I tell you the moon
Will heal all your diseases and solve every problem.
Just turn to the moon and it will stop them.
Use no herbs or ointments of any kind
If you have the moon as your only mind.
You are under life, truth and love,
Naked with the moon directly above.
I stay under the moon all the time
Or life wouldn't be worth a dime."

4 Other animals tried to stay under the moon all the time.
Life wasn't worth a dime,
For the moon always runs 'round the Earth once a day.
It's more easy by far just to pray.

5 And how do you stay naked all the time? You will get a sunburn.
Growled Millie, "No way!
It is easier for Wyatt Earp to get a gunburn."

6 "I was so mad that I saw purple
When I set eyes on Wyatt Earp,
El hombre who could never lose.
He set about like clockwork orange;
He tore the door right off the car hinge,
Because he was so angry at some Jose."

7 Animals were mesmerized when they heard all that jazz.
When they got sick, they turned to herbs, ointments and other
razzmatazz.

8 But some to the moon without ceasing appealed
And as a result they completely were healed.
Nothing they lacked,
Knowing this fact:
The moon is perfect when it sets,
Just as when it's above,
So animals below are perfect like Diana's love,
So animals enjoy good health through every joy-filled day,
But dressed in fear and ignorance, we seem the other way.

9 "One more thing", Millie growled. "Don't call the moon 'Diana';
Leave that name on an African banner
Off in the grasslands where lions dwell;
You can tell those devils by the smell.
If you yell out, 'Diana', the moon gets more bright?
The moon since bereshith has sent the same light."

10 "But Leo called her 'Diana", and he wasn't lying."

11 "But Leo was a lion!"

12 "Leo we must follow;
In his words we must wallow!"

13 "I'm afraid in my mouth is my foot
Just to sound cute
With my feline root
And my own horn to toot.
You may do as he says,
Not exactly what he says;
I guess that save our days."

14 "When offered water, drink; don't ask for wine;
Water is fine!

15 "When offered bread, don't ask for a stone,
Unless you eat bone.

16 "When you see a stone, don't call it bread,
unless you have rocks in the head!

17 "When told to jump off a cliff,
Turn up your paws at the weasel, biff, biff!

18 "When offered all in the world,
Don't take it unless by the moon,
Which is coming real soon!

19 "And don't walk on water;
Take a bird, a plane or a boat across
Or like lemmings, you march to the slaughter."

XXVI

1 A fox once began to bark
And a lot of animals began to listen.
His followers were called Shaky Barkers or Shakers,
Because he barked, "When I bark,
Not even Diana can shake my testimony!"

2 He barked, "Bark nothing but the truth
If you want to be a friend of Leo.
If a Shaker barks, it must be the truth
Or he is no friend of Leo.
A Shaker who is a friend of Leo must not swear by anything, even
Diana."

3 Many Cougars became Shakers,
But most of them followed the Poppa, Martin or the king of the
foxes.
So did coyotes among them who were less sincere.

4 Later, a coyote named Dick, who barked with the Shakers, rose to
become Grand Cougar.

5 While serving as Vicious Cougar, he had lost the election to a
pig named Jack.
Jack won a close election by promising to eliminate poverty in
North America.

6 Unfortunately, many pigs believed it necessary to exploit
animals overseas
To improve the standard of living in North America
And to keep other lands from being influenced by the bears and
other enemies.

7 Bears were despised
Because they preached in favor of equal division of property
between rich and poor animals.
Coyotes growled, "Listen not to the word of the bears
Who say better beasts shouldn't get their large shares."

8 A long, bloody war was started with gorillas in Southeast Asia,
When many North American Animals were sent there to impose a
government and economic system similar to that in North America,
Where rich pigs kept getting richer
While impoverished animals starved.
Animals that worked the hardest got the least in return.

9 Machinations of the wolves continued.
During wars, many of their leaders had been captured by the
Cougars and taken to North America.
Most of them went unpunished for their horrible crimes against
lions and other animals.
Their intelligence network remained in place.
This network included chimpanzees that did dirty work overseas.
Beside spying, they attempted to subvert and overthrow foreign
governments.

10 Their cousins, the coyotes in North America, were their best
students, even better than the kodiak grizzly bears.
As result of mutual contact with the wolves, coyotes cooperated
with kodiak grizzly bears to prevent any animals in the world from
electing leaders freely.

11 Coyotes pretended to continue a conflict with the bears,
And called opponents in North America "Bad News Bears."
Many animals were unjustly accused.
A phony war went on for years between North American animals
and the bears.

12 A coyote named Joe went around growling,
"Let's examine the government, splitting hairs,
Because the woods are crawling with Bad News Bears!"

13 Dick headed the Uncougar Activities Committee.
Many lost jobs after being slandered by Dick and Joe.
This made Dick so famous that he became Vicious Cougar
But afterward lost the election for Grand Cougar to Jack.

14 Coyotes became more and more displeased with Jack.
They kept howling, "What are we going to do about Jack?
We want our political power back.
Whenever from the White Tree he cavorts
With many strange females he consorts.
So many enemies he tries to please,
He is liable to disband our chimpanzees."

15 They sent a lynx named Lee to work among the bears.
He married a kodiak grizzly bear
And took her back with him to North America.

16 One day, the kodiak grizzly bear growled to her husband,
"Here in America, we have it made.
Go climb that tree and enjoy a parade.
If you climb sufficiently high,
You will see the Grand Cougar Jack go by."

17 A beaver nibbled at the branch of the tree where Lee sat,
So it collapsed when Jack strolled by,
And Lee fell almost on top of Jack,
While a coyote bit Jack from behind.

18 Coyotes kept pigs out of the way that would have protected Jack.
Pigs then had orders to kill Lee on sight.
Lee jumped and killed the first one that came after him.

19 Other pigs surrounded and captured Lee.
While Lee was held by coyotes,
A lion jumped and killed him,
So nobody could learn all the details of the case.
Coyotes hoped that Bad News Bears would be blamed.

20 Jack and his brothers enjoyed many wild orgies with females
Until tragedies struck.
One brother, Bobby, was trampled by a camel.
Another, Ted, lost public favor after a female was drowned in a
bay. Coyotes had killed her and blamed Ted for the murder.

21 Another pig named Lyndon became grand Cougar.
He sent many more to die in Southeast Asia.
Most of them were poor goats
Who lacked the means to avoid conscription.
Many kids protested.
Lyndon growled, "I can't run again with these pains in my head;
Elect the Vicious Cougar Hubie instead."

22 Goats bleated angrily around the cave where Hubie was being
nominated.
A gang of pigs clobbered the kids on the head,
Swinging wildly,
Injuring many innocent bystanders.
This inflamed all cougars against the pigs
And even more against the Norway rat, Hubie.
The cougars all voted for Dick instead.

23 Even though he was a Shaker,
Dick swore to be faithful when he took office.
Everybody believed him but he barked nothing but lies.
He broke his promise to end the war in Asia quickly.

24 There was a foul odor all over the North American forest.
Other animals sniffed around to find out what it was.
There stood skunks named Danny and Larry.

25 Danny and Larry moaned,
"Even worse than a pain in the belly,
Something goes on that is really smelly.
Dick and his band are really killers,
At war with orangutans as well as gorillas!"

26 Dick sent bats to spy on the skunks
To obtain information to prove that the skunks were bigger stinkers
than Dick.
A group of bats were trapped
While they flew in the dark, attempting to spy on Larry.
A black panther rolled a big rock in front of the cave
So that the bats could not escape.

27 There was a stampede of bison,
But Dick insisted that he would not be buffaloed.

28 He refused to resign, barking:
"I don't care what allegations the alligators cook;
I'm telling you, I am not a crook!
I want to make myself perfectly clear:
We'll be out of Asia, maybe next year."

29 Dick ordered eagles to blast the gorillas
Even while cougars were celebrating Leo's birthday.
Meanwhile, prairie dogs scurried in and out of their holes
Trying to keep from getting involved in the spying scandal.

30 Alligators accused Dick of other irregularities:
Cougars protecting Dick made improvements on his land at the
expense of the public.
Dick kept mink pelts and other presents from foreign kings.
Dick became very rich while in office,
But he failed to contribute the amount of pelts he was required to
help support the cougars' government,
Which was wasting the land's resources fighting Dick's war in Asia.

31 An aide in the White Birch Tree, named Alex, disclosed that
Dick kept parrots hidden there.
The parrots could repeat conversations between Dick and his aides,
But Dick fired all animals working in the White Tree that wanted to
cooperate with the investigation.
The alligators pressed the case,
And finally the badgers on the Supreme Court insisted that the
parrots be released.

32 Two of the parrots imitated Dick and an aide named Bob Cat.

33 "Squawk, the federal pigs will investigate."

34 "Have the chimpanzees stop them before it's too late.
We'll say it's a matter of feline security,
And after that no one will question our purity!
We need a plan that cannot fail
To get those jackasses out of jail."

35 "But pigs keep on squealing!", the squawking repeated.

36 "I said, call the chimps now, you (expletive deleted)!"

37 "But what about bats that are locked in their cages?"

38 "Here are nice bugs to feed them to silence their rages.
Go wash the bugs clean now as does the raccoon,
And then we'll be pure as the light of the moon."

39 This disclosure caused Dick to lose all support
And he quit his office.

40 A jackass took Dick's place as Grand Cougar.
He had been appointed Vicious Cougar by Dick,
Because the hippopotamus elected to that office had been forced to
quit earlier.

41 The jackass tenderly forgave Dick with Diana directly overhead.
He forgave Dick for everything he had done while he was Grand
Cougar,
Even though Dick had attempted to eliminate the last vestiges of
freedom enjoyed under the cougars' constitution.

42 He brayed, "Hyaw, Leo said the merciful are all that can be
winners,
For he loved everyone, even Republicans and sinners."

43 After several years, all cougars loved and forgave Dick.
If we remember correctly,
Dick finally became Grand Cougar again,
Even though he had already been elected twice,
Which was the legal limit.
The elephants never forget,
But this is information they refuse to leak;
They refuse to talk about sex, religion or politics.
Giraffes refuse to talk, taking the fifth amendment.
Let's just hope Dick didn't screw everybody again.

XXVII

1 All North American animals were dismayed
Because they were stuck with a stupid jackass for a Grand Cougar.

2 The cougars finally left Southeast Asia.
The jackass ordered cougars to snatch all baby gorillas they could bring back
So families could adopt them in North America.
Many baby gorillas died on the way
As result of the rough ride in the claws of eagles that carried them.

3 The jackass lost patience quickly
When orangutans held some cougars hostage,
When the cougars were caught swimming off the Asian coast,
Attempting to spy on the orangutans.
Cougars invaded Asia,
And orangutans put up fierce resistance.
A greater number of cougars were killed
Than the number of hostages rescued.

4 All animals sent meat to support the government.
One year, surplus meat was refunded to all the animals,
No longer sent to ones fighting in Southeast Asia.
The jackass planned to refund meat mainly to the rich
And let the poor continue to starve.
The congregation of geese could not put up with that.
They apportioned the refunds according to the wishes of the public.

5 The jackass brayed, "I had to consent to the Cong Geese's judgament
Which they kept insisting without any budgement."

6 The jackass feared an epidemic of fleas.
Swine were most susceptible.
He ordered all animals bitten to keep them from catching fleas.
There was no epidemic of fleas anywhere in the world, even among swine,
And some cougars became sick with rabies as a result of the bites.

7 His last act in office was a proposal that a small island
crowded with cockroaches become part of the cougars' territory with
full representation in their government.
He growled, "No other creature is fairer to me.
I keep them as pets in the white birch tree!"

8 Even after he left office,
The jackass enjoyed playing games
Kicking a little ball in some holes.
His aim was so bad
That many animals were injured,
Hit in the head by errant balls.

XXVIII
(Aleph)
1 The next Grand Cougar purred only "meow" (moral equivalent of
war) when there was an energy shortage.
Many animals froze,
Because they had no warm place to hibernate in the Winter.

2 Some pigs used all the energy they wanted
No matter how much the rhinoceros charged.
The rhinoceros was very dangerous,
Causing deadly explosions, radiation and pollution.
The pigs did not care,
As long as they could live like kings,
selling and using the energy.

3 A skunk named Karen complained,
"Nobody should work where rhinoceri are stored.
Several times myself I was gored."

4 She ran down the road, making a big stink.
Look out, Karen!
She was trampled to death by an elephant.

(Beth)
5 Kangaroos hopped over to North America,
Publishing and filming garbage
And ripping off the cougars.
They controlled the gnus completely
That carried information about current events.
They threw platypus eggs, smearing many upstanding cougars.
The dumped grease and other garbage in lakes,
Making an icky film on the surface of the water.
These were disgusting pictures indeed!
A lot of real boars passed for entertainment.

6 Cougars were gullible enough to elect one of those boars to be
Grand Cougar.
Bears eagerly agreed to a treaty with the boar, limiting all arms,
Knowing that he would allow the North American environment to be
wrecked, and the poor would stay uneducated and unproductive.

7 That boar often slept--no one overworked him;
Between naps, his eagles smashed camels that irked him,
To make sure they were left with nothing but sand;
They conflicted with lions for the same land.

8 There were two other boars, both named John.
One sang songs
And the other made films that favored peace and freedom.
They were both murdered.
A hole was ripped in one,
And the other was bitten by a poisonous snake.
Both deeds were pulled off by coyotes,
Who brainwashed perverted goats into doing the dirty work,
So nobody blamed the vicious cougar, George, or any other coyotes.

9 A bitch coyote named Anita howled,
"Bring down the maximum wrath of the law,
If one male holds another male's paw!"

10 As result, any animal applying for any position had to answer
all kinds of questions about their past background.
Even butterflies had to describe what they like as caterpillars.
Many animals were driven off,
Accused of sympathizing with the bears.
Koalas in Australia were decimated almost out of existence.

11 Cougars considered themselves the most fervent followers of Leo.
They were easily misled by Coyotes.
Coyotes attempted to seize power by taking positions as spiritual leaders. They growled:
"No animal can see Diana's face,
Unless cougars dominate every other race."

12 Many wolves who escaped retribution after their vicious war
Set up tyrannical governments that oppressed South American Jaguars.
Those governments cooperated with the most evil plots of the coyotes.

13 A coyote named Jim went about preaching,
"All who don't believe in me will have to run
Because greater than Diana, I am number one!"

14 Jim built a corral in South America
And led many animals there.
Most of those animals were North American black panthers.
They were all poisoned at a water hole;
Thus a program of genocide was begun against black panthers.

15 Arose the worst of the coyotes, named George.
He growled, "I must have full control of our foreign affairs,
To protect all beasts in all lands from the bears!"

16 Nobody knew what was going on in the world,
As George pushed the congregation of geese to pass new laws.
All intelligence and other covert activities of coyotes in North America and chimpanzees overseas had to be kept top secret.

17 George rose to become Vicious Cougar and sought higher office.
He attempted to bushwhack the cougars' constitution,
So that none would be free to express themselves,
Especially if they bring to light the coyotes' nefarious plots.

18 Monkey business by the chimpanzees was directed especially against llamas west of the Andes in South America.
Their leader Sal distributed meat to keep the population well fed.
The chimpanzees whispered to the llamas,
"If you have problems, your leader doesn't care
Because Sal is really a Bad News Bear!"
Llamas trampled on Sal and installed a tapir pig in his place.
The tapir pig ended the food program as he favored other rich pigs.

19 There was much fighting in Central America.
As rebels tried to overthrow a government that intended to feed all their animals.
Jaguars bargained among themselves, trying to make peace
But George met with the rebels to keep the war going.

20 The North American Cong Geese
Made it illegal to send meat to the rebels,
But coyotes sent meat to the rebels in violation of the law.

21 Coyotes even maintained puppet governments in parts of Asia,
Making special deals with pet tigers including Sun Dung Moon and Mark Fernando.
Sun Dung Moon moved to North America.
He growled, "Forget about Leo; I am your Lord;
Follow me and keep your life free from discord!"
He became very rich,
Exploiting kids who worked for him without pay.

(Gimel) 22 It took a great deal of wealth to influence the congregation of geese and Grand Cougar.
Candidates for office had to spend a lot for the opportunity
To honk out to the public
To make themselves known
And the put down their opponents.
To stay in office
They had to give more and more to fat pigs
And take everything away from others and make them starve.

23 Animals all over the world sharpened their fangs and claws, preparing for war,
Because the pigs hogged most of the world's scarcening resources.

(Daled)
24 A studious wolf named Sigmund barked learned discourses about the minds of all animals.
He defined some thinking as pathological that should be forcibly treated and changed.
Many other wolves and lions acquired degrees of higher learning, putting them in position to perpetuate this fraud.
They could growl about any animal,
Claiming that its mind was sick.
They corralled dissidents
And had them bitten by poisonous snakes to weaken them
So that they would not carry out activities to improve the government.

25 There were many starving and homeless animals,
But all that was offered them was incarceration.
Lions devoted much of their resources to Sigmund's projects,
So Lions helped nobody any more, not even other lions.

26 The lions claimed to be the most generous animals.
They had always shared food with other animals to show their love for Diana.
As result of Leo's preachings,
All animals were supposed to share food with impoverished and sick animals.

27 Unfortunately, a few animals owned the lion's share of property and special privileges.

XXIX
1 Cougars made trouble in Western Asia to get control of rhinos that provided energy.
Cougars maintained a tyrannical king over the tigers.
The tigers clawed and bit to remove him.
The king had allowed rich subjects to be entertained by indecent shows,
While letting poor camels starve.
He tortured many dissidents.

2 The king was driven away to be replaced by a devout worshiper of Dialla
Who was called the Diallatollah.
He and his band fought back against the cougars,
Capturing many of them and keeping them corralled for months.

3 Musk oxen by the Euphrates river were enemies of the tigers.
 Cougars provided food to the oxen and sharpened their tusks
To send them to war against the tigers,
Who had grabbed cougars and kept them hostages.
The oxen had a leader who was even more brutal.

4 The oxen bleated:
"Forever may our leader reign; Without him we don't know who's sane.
Against our enemies we slam;
They find no one who give saddam!"

5 The Diallatollah growled,
Though tigers constantly growl and holler
The oxen won't faithfully worship Dialla!
The tigers fought the oxen to a stalemate.

6 The boar serving as Grand Cougar secretly sent aid to the tigers, as the tigers sent meat to aid rebels in Central America.

7 The war left the oxen with little to eat.
They had to get food by renting out rhinos
That all animals needed for energy.
They had to compete with pigs nearby who rent them out for very little.
Those pigs were led by a rich Amir.
Pigs in North America urged them to compete unfairly
To undercut the oxen.
The Grand Cougar George had been planning for years for a war with the oxen to get control of the rhinos.

8 The oxen jumped the pigs and forced out the Amir.
They had learned from the cougars
That one could jump smaller and weaker animals
And get away with it.

9 Conflicts between cougars and bears ended in time
So that the coyote, George, could concentrate on the oxen.
George was very angry that oxen jumped the pigs.
He growled at the oxen,
"With you I have to pick a bone
If you don't leave the pigs alone."

10 Saddam growled, "Don't dare talk to me so rude.
By lions, camels still are chewed!"

11 A costly conflict was begun.
Finally a conference was called,
Keeping lions away from the camels
And keeping oxen from taking control of all the rhinos.

12 George was elected Grand Cougar after growling to the others:
I don't want to lay any bad trips
By raising taxes; read my lips!

13 George broke that promise and raised taxes soon after taking office.
That made many rich pigs angry and they refused to vote for him again.

14 George lost in his bid for reelection.

15 A son of George was the worst;
He stole two elections to be Grand Cougar.

16 Pigs were delighted because Shrub promised to cut taxes to be even less than they were before.

17 His brother, Jeb, ran a Southeastern peninsula and helped him steal the votes there.
Black panthers were blocked from voting.
They were charged falsely with past crimes.

18 Most lions intended to vote against Shrub,
But animals were confused by illegal ballots.
So by mistake, lions voted for a jackal who kept growling,
"Against the establishment we must fight
Because we know that Dolf was right."

19 Ballots in that peninsula had to be bitten to indicate the vote.
Some ballots had rotten wood that could not be bitten cleanly
by old infirm lions.
Cougars could not reliably count the votes as the ballots passed through the Cougars' claws.

20 A bitch coyote named Katherine served as Secretary of State for that peninsula.

21 She was quick to certify Shrub as the winner of the election

22 All ballots in the region were being recounted,
But corrupt badgers on the Supreme Court growled,
"Before opposition to Shrub can mount,
We order that region to stop the count!"

23 Katherine promised election reforms:
In another election four years later,
Animals could indicate their votes
By poking the backs of monkeys.
The monkeys swung by vines to counting stations where the votes
were counted.

24 Shrub gathered the monkeys and dangled bananas in front of
them.
He growled, "I need you now to save the day;
Here are nice bananas for votes my way!"
Monkey's relayed the votes falsely.
Many votes for the opponent were cast for Shrub.

25 Eagles smashed into trees killing thousands of cougars there.
Cougars were angry, looking for someone to blame.
Who else but the musk oxen?
Shrub warred with oxen for years and many animals were killed.

26 Shrub failed to maintain beavers that would have built dams to
protect the Gulf coast.
A storm drowned many animals there
As Shrub failed to help evacuate them.

27 For many years, many pigs banded together as corporations to
provide food and other goods to the public.
More and more, corporations took advantages of loopholes in the
law to acquire great wealth.

28 After Shrub was installed as Grand Cougar by corrupt badgers, he
appointed two new badgers to the Supreme Court.

29 Those badgers insisted that corporations be allowed to contribute an unlimited amount to political campaigns.

30 This granted corporations great influence over the Congregation of geese and other representatives.

31 The pigs ran candidates in primary elections against any of the Cong geese that opposed them.

32 Under Shrub's administration, corporations went as far as writing the laws,
Allowing the pigs to get richer and richer, leaving others with nothing.

33 Corporations even controlled the monkeys
Who made sure that all elections went in favor of their candidates.

34 Because of cutbacks in government support, raccoons stopped gathering food properly and many animals starved.

35 The public was so sick of misrule that they bucked corporate power for two elections.

36 Imagine their consternation when a black panther was elected grand cougar!

37 Coyotes tried everything: stealing elections, shutting down the government, defaulting on debts in attempts to regain power.

38 The black panther had to be the greatest grand cougar to withstand such onslaught.

39 Even pigs could no longer put up with those coyotes.
They squealed, We've had enough of your kinds of abusers
Please harken to us, the great wealth producers!

XXX

1 A few pigs owned all the land and nearly all the meaty rumps.
Rabbits, goats, black panthers and other oppressed animals were
left with nothing, not even land on which to graze.
They were stirred to quite a craze.
What little they had was for others to rob;
For many goats, that was their only job.
Because so deeply they felt cheated,
They got together and moaned and bleated,
"Corral those pigs in garbage dumps!"

2 Angry pigs started to clobber kids on the heads again.
The angry bleating of goats, camels and other oppressed animals all
over the world was heard,
Drowning out the loudest chirps of any bird;
Their emaciated faces were a sight,
But they were charged with being reds again.
This led to rampages by the pigs, whose opponents were slaughtered
left and right.

3 A lion who called himself Chairman preached the words of Leo to
the oppressed animals, who decided never to claw or bite back.
They refused to cooperate with the pigs, who no longer could
benefit by using them.
Thus those oppressed returned a far more mighty smack,
And in no way abusing them.

4 They used a plan that never fails:
Other animals refused to help the pigs curl their tails.
Oink! Who heard of pigs with straight tails?
And they refused to supply mud.
Clean pigs are no good.

5 The pigs gave in to each demand.
Other animals were given back their land,
Resulting in more freedom for all.
And all, both big and small, began to have a ball.

6 While aardvarks looked on all this with askance;
They were always content to eat nothing but ants.

XXXI

1 On top of Mt. Victoria, Leo kept roaring:
"Diana! Diana!, every time the moon soared above the horizon.
The moon shone more bright than ever.

2 Then Diana finally spoke:
"Go down and take all animals to the garden of paradise.
There will be no sin, disease death, sorrow or crying in any land."

3 Leo went down roaring to all the beasts.
Some thought it was just a joke.
Some followed, not even needing a poke.
Some just listened.
None could fight him.

4 Then all animals looked with wonder;
The sun disappeared; it began to thunder,
And the moon began to shine very bright.
Every creature was amazed by the sight.

5 Many a pig
Thought itself too big.
They refused to leave
On apocalypse eve
And leave behind
The things on their mind:
Their riches and lust,
So afraid things would rust.

6 They squealed, "Hyenas will laugh
To hear such chaff!"

7 Because of the sin
That the pigs were stuck in,
They suffered for years
Down in dirt to their ears;
They had to wallow,
Before they would follow
And dance and sing
In the path of their king.

8 And hyenas marched on to the land of peace
Although their laughter couldn't cease.

9 And when ostriches heard Leo talking,
They stayed behind and
Kept their heads in the sand,
But it soon was their turn
For their tails to burn,
And oven ostriches followed squawking.

10 Not for a second halted a muscle;
Even two-toed sloths had to hustle.

11 Opossums were hung
By the tail from a rung.
Down pointed the head
As they all played dead.
So great was their zeal,
That every one stayed dead for real.

12 Monkeys thought it was all in fun;
They chased the weasels, every one,
All around with a frantic rush.
They never stopped
Till the weasels popped,
All around the mulberry bush.

13 And lo! A Miracle! There were all animals that ever followed
Leo faithfully, loving Diana and all other animals.
Those who had died arose and joined the others.
All followers of Leo went to the garden of paradise,
Where the moon is always full.

14 All that followed had eternal bliss,
Just as if they could feel not a thing but a kiss.
No more sin, disease, death, sorrow or crying or kvetching or
sighing for any,
They could all live like kings without needing a penny.

XXXII

1 The leaders of the bears told them not to go.

2 We share all rumps and carcassky equally.
We enjoy eternal blisska with no private propersky.
You should listen to Leonid not Leo!"

3 Bears claimed that the were trying to help other animals divide
land more equally.
Some wild asses in central Asian mountains rebelled against a
government imposed by the bears.
Thousands of bears marched into their land to take control.
Driven by Hammy, the wild asses kicked like mad,
Because the bears tried to stop them from braying to Hammy five
times a day.

4 The tigers were reluctant to follow.
They had been in constant conflict with the wolves, foxes and
cougars,
Who claimed to follow Leo
And wanted to import some rhinos from Asia.

5 Tigers were angry, condemning the aggression against others who
followed Hammy.
Cougars were afraid that the bears would take control of Asian
rhinos
That the cougars wanted to harness for energy.

6 There was the threat of world-wide devastation
Because of conflicts between bears, tigers and cougars.
They threatened to unleash Godzilla and other dinosaurs against
each other.
The bears had one that weighed one hundred megatons.

7 A few animals followed Leo faithfully, loving all others.
They prevented all-out war.
Finally, the smiling face of the moon made it clear
That dinosaurs were extinct.

8 From plaintive bears were heard these cries:
"We will listen no more to your lies!"
With longing for freedom in every heart,
Even kodiak grizzly bears split apart.

9 Most bears followed Leo, thinking that their leaders had always
lied to them.
Anyone could see that party members enjoyed extra wealth and
privileges.
Eventually, even the leaders followed Leo,
Because there was no one else left.

10 The panda bears in East Asia were also reluctant to follow Leo.

11 The chairman of the pandas growled,
"We gettee impelialists off our backs;
Now we chink away at our mountain yaks!"

12 Finally Asian leaders including the Chairman, Buddy, Hammy
and Krishna followed Leo, taking the others with them,
Because Leo said the same things that they always did.

XXXIII

1 This left the lions in the grasslands.
A disease spread around them called rabies--a serious disease.
It is so bad that it even talks.

2 The rabies said, "We are king of the beasts.
We follow nobody except Diana.

3 "Do you remember when we were slaves on the Nile,
Forced to catch fish for the cruel crocodile?

4 "Diana sent a whale named Moby Dick,
Who turned sticks into snakes, which was quite a trick.
Attracted at first by a big burning bush,
He then jumped away and did not burn his tush.
He then did the number on Faggio's crocs.
(You must take this garbage right now as ad hocs)
Number ten wiped out their number one whelp;
Everyone ran around screaming for help.
The lions passed over by mammoth stampedes,
That killed off the first of all crocodile breeds.
Then Faggio said, 'Moby you better go!'
Said Moby, 'We lions are happy to blow!'

5 "Moby took us South,
But we were blocked by Ethiopian mountains.
The crocodiles chased after us.
Diana caused a great quake,
And the mountains opened up.
We passed through and settled in the grassland.

6 "Moby went up Mount Victoria and spouted toward Diana.
Diana gave him ten commandments..."

XXXIV

1 "There is no moon except Diana;
From any other moon, you will not even get a banana.

2 Diana is so lovely a portrait, no artist can draw;
If you want to eat, you will just have to gobble her raw.

3 Don't say Diana unless you expect her to help you;
Say anything else and she'll say you're a miserable whelp you,
And don't call Diana the moon;
If you do it will crash very soon.

4 Every week on the seventh do nothing at all,
Because that is the day we lions Diana must call.

5 Every lion must honor his mamma and poppa,
Or he's a baboon or a rat or a wolf or improppa.

6 No animal, any other animal ever may kill.
Don't argue with me, for that is Diana's will.

7 Throughout all its seasons, each beast should keep only one
mate,
Or else by our great moon, Diana, no creature can rate.

8 No beast from any ass its rump may take,
Or else by Diana you're making a big mistake.

9 Don't chatter about any other unless it is true,
Or Diana's finger will tell you just what to do.

10 Don't even think about grabbing a rump or a tail,
Or else in Diana's book you are certain to fail.

CONCLUSION: You animals will have to keep singing 'til
everything's right,
Or the next time you see her, Diana's a terrible sight."

XXXV

1 "Only these commandments obey;
They are our courage and they are our stay.
We don't bite off the rump; that is dirty, treyf;
We must eat the whole carcass, when served by the chef.
In the grassland we must remain
As rain in the plain out in Spain.
We must wait until Diana herself tells us when a king should lead
us into the garden.
Only she is our warden!"

2 All other animals left--
This made the lions all feel bereft.
The lions really began to pout
When they looked at the sky and the moon was put out.
An anguished moan went forth form their lips
When the moon went permanently in eclipse.

3 The lions all roared, "Oy vey!
What can we say?
Adonai lo!
Why didn't we go?
Where are all the other animals
To supply us, cannibals?
There is nothing to eat
For love of Pete!
Not even camels left to devour;
This we fear is our most horrid hour!"

4 And the lions all starved to death;
If you say that is bad, I can only lithp, "Yeth!"

Appendix

I:5-6 Isa 7:14
II:4 Matt 1:20-25
:6 Matt 2:1-2,9-11
:12 Matt 2:16
III:1 Luke 1
:2-5 Matt 3
IV:1-2 Matt 4:18-19
:8-10 Matt 16:13-18
:12-14 Matt 26:34
V:2 John 2:1-10
:3 Matt 4:1-11
:9 Matt 14:25-31
:12-16 Luke 17:12-19
:17-20 Mark 7:25-30
VI John 8:3-11
VII Matt 26:21-25
VIII:6 Luke 22:47-51
:12 Luke 22:54-62
:18 Matt 27:3-5
IX Matt 27
X:4-16 John 20:24-29
XI Acts 2:1-6
XII Acts 6-Acts 8
XIII Acts 9
XIV:7 Col 3:2
:8-10 Acts 17-23
:18-21 Acts 19:13-16
XV Peter was considered the first Pope after he was crucified
upside down.
XVI:7 Charlemagne was king of the Franks
:8 Prophet Mohammed founded Islam
:12 Crusades attempted to capture Holy Land
XVII Martin Luther broke with the Pope
:11 Famous painting: Massacre at St. Bartholomew

XIX1 King John in England
:10 Joan of Arc led French army
:11 King Henry VIII of England broke with Pope
:13-15 King Charles I was beheaded
:15 Oliver Cromwell ruled as Lord Protector
:18 Ireland rebelled and broke from U.K.
:21-25 George Washington led colonial army and was first U.S.
president.
:27-28 Abraham Lincoln was President during Civil War

:29 Ulysses Grant led Union army
XX French Revolution Deposed monarchy
:5 Jacobin leader, Robespierre was guillotined
:6 Jean Paul Marat was stabbed in bathtub
:7 Napoleon became emperor, set up Napoleonic Code.
:13 Russian Revolution deposed Czar
:14 White Russians supported counterrevolution.
KGB is Soviet intelligence network
XXII Adolf Hitler was chancellor of Germany
:23 Mussolini, dictator of Italy, invaded Ethiopia
:28 Germany invaded Poland and the lowlands
:29 Battle of Britain
:30 Winston Churchill was Prime Minister of Britain
:31 Switzerland stayed out of the war
:32 Germany invaded Russia
:34 Japan expanded its empire
:35 Harry Truman was U.S. President
:36 U.S. dropped atomic bombs on two Japanese cities
:37 Germany and Austria were partitioned
:38 First Arab-Israeli war was in 1948
:39 Separate treaty between Egypt and Israel
XXIII Jehovah's Witnesses sell Awake and Watchtower door to door.
XXIV Joseph Smith founded Latter Day Saints (Called Mormons)

XXVI:1 George Fox founded Quakers
:4 Richard Nixon was 37th President
:5 John F. Kennedy, 35th President sent advisors to Vietnam.
:12 Joseph McCarthy investigated loyalty in the Senate
:13 Nixon was on House Unamerican Activities Committee
:15-19 Lee Harvey Oswald Married Marina in Soviet Union. He was accused of assassinating President Kennedy.
:21 Lyndon B. Johnson was 36th President
:22 Hubert Humphrey was Vice President. Police rioted at 1968 Democratic convention.
:24 Larry O'Brien was chairman of Democratic Committee
Daniel Elsberg released Pentagon Papers.
:26 Cubans were caught breaking into Democratic headquarters in Watergate Hotel
:31 Alexander Butterfield disclosed tapes of White House conversations.
:40-42 Gerald Ford, 38th President, pardoned Nixon for all acts as President.
XXVII:2 Vietnamese babies were flown to U.S. when Americans left Vietnam.
:3 Crew of U.S. ship Mayaguez was taken hostage by Cambodia.
:4-5 Congress passed income tax rebate

:6 President Ford provided for free flu shots
:7 He proposed statehood for Puerto Rico
:8 He used a club to play golf
XXVIII: 1 Jimmy Carter was 39th President of the United States
:3 Karen Silkwood worked at nuclear power plant
:5 Australian, Rupert Murdock founded publishing empire
Grease was a hit movie, though panned by critics
6 Ronald Reagan was 40th President
:7 Jim Jones founded Jonestown colony in Guyana
:8 John Beluchi died of a drug overdose
John Lennon, one of the Beattles, was assassinated
:9 Anita Bryant lead an anti-gay crusade
:13 Jim Jones ran a colony in Guyana
:15 George Herbert Walker Bush was a Vice President and President
:18 Salvadore Allende was overthrown in Chile
Daniel Ortega was a President of Nicaragua
:21 Ferdinand Marcos was a President of the Philippines
Sun Myung Moon was a religious leader from Korea
:24 Sigmund Freud began psychoanalysis
XXIX:
:1 Shah was overthrown in Iran
:4 Saddam Hussein was President of Iraq
:14 George W. Bush was 43rd President of the United States
:31 Barack Obama was 44th President
XXXII
:3 Soviet Union intervened in Afghanistan
:10 China put down rebellion in Tibet
XXXIII See Exodus

THE LAZY KING

With joy all the animals started to sing;
They elected the lion to be their king;
He would make sure there was enough food for all
And see that the leaves were removed in the fall,
But no matter how subjects continued to rave,
Their king stayed curled up asleep in his cave,
Until one day when it came to pass
That the hawks had inspected the holy blue grass,
That was planted to signify that all agree
That animals should roam around free,
Many animals then went hog wild
That the special area was defiled!
They caught the culprit that everyone hated,
Who on the turf, red, white and blue urinated!
The lion's loud roaring the forest stilled:
He ordered that the offender be killed,
And broke his neck with a single leap;
Then the lion curled up and went back to sleep!
They weren't even allowed to brood,
As many animals went without food!
Large beasts continued to prey on the the small
And no leaves were ever removed in the fall!

LAZY KING GEORGE II

Large beasts continued to prey on the small,
And no leaves were ever removed in the fall;
Thus, did the lion continue to bungle,
Neglecting all the affairs in the jungle,
Until finally reached him the ominous word,
So the big chance arrived so that he could be heard:
In the desert were camels by tigers attacked,
So the lions were called on to lead with a pact.
Around them did elephants and rhinos gather,
As a bird went squawking around named D. Rather.
Of the foreign issue was such a big schpiel,
All forgot the misdeeds of a cub named Prince Neil,
So King George lead the others to march to the East,
Proving lions should reign over every other beast,
And victory came after a mighty struggle,
Though tigers are nothing with which one should snuggle,
But when winning troops returned home all they found
Was more devastation for miles around,
For no matter how valiant warriors bled,
They did not make sure animals home would be fed.

THE CLEVER FOX

Around a farm a wily fox once crept;
In a coop called the Constitution, chickens were kept.
He had a clever plan to do them harm,
By running to be president of the farm--
That proved to be the perfect solution,
After vowing to protect, preserve and defend the Constitution!

THE FOX-CHICKEN PAX

The chickens wanted to come to no harm
If they went about pecking all over the farm.
The foxes all by dismay there were stricken
By the terrible squawking when they grabbed a chicken;
Because of that, all their pleasures were curbed
By guard dogs when they heard the chickens disturbed.
To many on both sides it would be fine
If when they get together, a treaty they sign.
The voices of all the chickens were raised:
They all started clucking, Allah be praised!
The foxes were just as pleased as them:
They started growling, Baruch hashem!
Representatives chosen, the meeting was good:
The Chicken Liberation Organization and the fox Likud.
The foxes complained that they couldn't stand
The CLO; they growled that it should be banned!
At the meeting the foxes allowed only those
Among the chickens that the foxes chose:
Those that were distributed extra feed
By foxes and so were misled by greed.
To reach an agreement with them was not hard,
So that over the chickens, a fox would stand guard.
No disturbance occurred on a single day
As the chickens were gradually carried away,
And thus the chickens were through as a group,
And all the foxes enjoyed chicken soup.

ANIMAL FUNNY FARM

The lion, the bear and the fox got together and decided to build a psychiatric ward in which to put the other animals. The lion, by virtue of his position as king of the beasts, claimed to be the psychiatrist. The fox was to be a nurse, and the bear would be an aide.

"It's about time something was done about all the psychotic animals in this jungle", said the bear. "For example, you heard the hyena's crazy laugh.

"He's clearly schizophrenic!", pronounced the lion.

"The rabbit hops away like mad whenever i approach!," said the Fox. "Jeez, is he terribly paranoid!"

"Do you see the way the opossum hangs by his tail for hours, without moving?, said the psychiatrist. "He must be catatonic!"

"I thought you were a cat yourself!" quipped the fox.

"Come on, cut the wise cracks!," roared the lion.

The consultation was shortly concluded, the ward was prepared and the inmates were brought in.

After a while, the fox spoke up. "It isn't right to keep all these poor sick animals here. We've got to help them!"

"What they need is tooth therapy!", the psychiatrist decided. "Let's get to work with our teeth!"

RACHEL AND RUFUS

The parents of Rachel the Rabbit were dismayed by her behavior.

"What should be done about Rachel?", Mrs Rabbit asked Mr. Rabbit. "She has no friends among other young rabbits. And what is worse, all her friends are raccoons, and she keeps getting closer to a male named Rufus!"

"I've heard of a notable Psychiatrist named Frederick the Fox.", Mr. Rabbit decided. "Let's take Rachel to consult with him.

The rabbit family met together in the office of Frederick. The psychiatrist told the family his conclusion at the end of their first session.

"It seems as if Rachel is very neurotic. This case will be difficult, but I can handle it if your family comes to my office for family therapy, for weekly sessions. More important, I must start chomp treatments right away!"

After saying that, he bit off Rachel's left rear leg and ate it up. By next week Rachel seemed much improved. She could hardly get around to see her racoon friends. At the conclusion of the second session a Frederick's office, he bit off her right rear leg. After that Rachel was more remarkably improved. She could hardly get around at all.

After about two months of therapy there was nothing left of Rachel at all.

Made in the USA
Charleston, SC
09 June 2014